ZIKR

ZIKR

POEMS BY

SAALEHA IDREES BAMJEE

UHLANGA

2018

Zikr

Published in Cape Town, South Africa by uHlanga in 2018

UHLANGAPRESS.CO.ZA

Distributed outside South Africa by the African Books Collective

AFRICANBOOKSCOLLECTIVE.COM

ISBN: 978-0-620-80325-0

Edited by Nick Mulgrew

Cover photograph by Saaleha Idrees Bamjee
Cover design and typesetting by Nick Mulgrew

The body text of this book is set in Garamond Premier Pro 11PT on 15PT

Some of the poems in this collection were first published in the following journals
and publications: *Poetry Potion, Badilisha Poetry X-Change, Mail & Guardian,
Ons Klyntji, The Sol Plaatje European Union Poetry Anthologies, New Coin,
New Contrast, Aerodrome,* and *loop.* The author would like to thank
the editors of these publications.

ACKNOWLEDGEMENTS

My mother for her voice. My father for this chin and for leaving behind a door to South African poetry by way of a circa-1970 edition of *Ophir*. My husband for insisting. Robert Berold for his remarkable ear for rhythm and line-breaks. Nick Mulgrew for his instinct. My dear friends for sharing, commenting on, liking and cheerleading every single piece I've ever put out there.

– S.I.B.

CONTENTS

My grandmother breaks her hip

My grandmother says we've brought her here to die.
Her broken bone picks under our fingernails,
a splintered stick splitting the tissue-beds, prying us apart.
We give her pills for our pain. Her cataracts cloud over her,
but she can see old blood on the ceiling of the state hospital.

My mother is wrung out; the guilt stretches across her bed,
nesting on sheets of the unsigned hospital plan.
The doctor at the clinic tells my uncle hip operations
cost hundreds of thousands; old people don't make it that far.
My mother says we've put a price on my grandmother.

My father finds a tumour

The herbalist told my mother to put a pumpkin
on the roof of our house – not just any gourd,
but one that had been prayed over, a vegetable effigy
of the thing in my father's brain.

You will see it shrink, he said, then your husband will get better.
So on went the pumpkin and the chemotherapy.
My father lost his hair, his sense of time,
and with each day in the sun, the pumpkin changed colours.

It never rotted, hardening into a lumpy stone on our roof.
At some point it just rolled off. In an unrelated event,
my father died from the complications of his cancer.

Kisses

I remember the first. The awkward insistence,
the disappointment no one writes about,
squashed against a cold car next to the track at Wits
while everyone else crammed for exams.

>Let me tell you something, don't kiss anyone
>just because you want it to be over with.
>That type of kiss you'll never get over.

The second one was more considerate.
He'd had much practice. It cost twenty rand to buy
the silence of the maid hoovering close to the couch.
The third was to prove I felt nothing, in the pitch of a car park.

>But then there was the one who kissed me as dismissal.
>His tongue sliced me, then left me in ribbons
>to clot in the seat of an empty theatre.

I cannot eat dates without wondering

I usually feel warm at a funeral, watching
the black cloaks of the mourning women
enveloping their embraces on the thin grey blankets
spread around the coffin, their febrile tears dissolving
tightly-fisted wads of pink and white tissue.

But the first funeral was cold.
I look back to the camphor and calico,
my father anointed and wrapped like an offering.
The final kiss on stiff lips. On his eyebrows.
crystals of evergreen frost.

My mother too young, far away in another room,
her world tossed into a corner. Always in the aftermath of sorrow,
guests are fed, blankets folded, furniture stacked,
prayer books piled up. And those date pits we saved
to tally our missives to the dead, and to God,

return to their plastic buckets.

Losing

Every night is an accounting:
one hundred calories in the breakfast banana;
the egg-white omelette makes up three hundred;
two hundred and fifty in the soup (with croutons);
four hundred portioned for supper;
tea plain and black before bed.

Before I sleep I then take stock
of every single step,
the minutes on the treadmill
I have done to outrun myself.
Every night I weigh up
how much I'll be worth in the end.

We are building your house

We are oiling skins for the stretch.
The vanities of breasts have been packed
away at the bottom of the lingerie drawer.
I am ready for your maps; silver borders
you will draw across belly and back.

I am ready for your words and the recipes
you will teach my grandchildren.
I have meal plans and itineraries.
We will visit museums.
You will learn to read music.

I have blocks for your cities
and paint for your worlds.
I have cleared a space in my mind, child,
in my waking hours, and in my heart.
We are framing your memories, and waiting.

Blighted ovum

Nobody answers when the doctor knocks.
After a week we return to an empty room,
the walls crumpling, the beginnings of rust.
We must raze it to the ground, scrape out its ruins.

I am on the table counting to nothing from ten.
But when I get there my mouth still holds
this ungifted name, its wrappings picked at,
edges smouldering to flakes by the flames.

After a miscarriage

It is all for the mother:
the glossed eyes, the quiver at the edge
of condolence. (There are biscuits
for the mourners.)

The door to the nursery is closed.
The talk is of other things
but for that one aunt puncturing
her sympathy with needles.

Have another soon, it will be good for you.
The father slips out to hold
his nose to the resolute blankness
of the baby wrap.

My grandmother leaves a voicemail

You're always busy, you never phone.
Crepe paper hands tap-tap the receiver
against her ear. I hear that metronome of age.
Through the line I listen to her record
of the frail betrayal of nerves:
the pain in her knees, her back,
oh, now also in her fingers –
all those weary places. Wearier still
without me, the granddaughter
always too busy to give her a call.

Until one afternoon, when there's
canned pilchard curry cooking
at the neighbours and I remember:
after-school buttered toast,
sugar in the inkomazi,
muskaana biscuits hot from the oven,
onions and cloves colouring the oil –
and a generous unshakable woman.
Then I phone my grandmother
and ask for the recipe.

Morning

Before the birds is the ebb-less tide of the highway.
I am just far enough away for the sound to be pleasant,
swathed in goose down, Egyptian cotton and electric blanket,
close to the hoarseness of the hadedas and the twisting calls
of a songbird I cannot name.

The day is just about to glow. Across the road,
men are arriving for morning prayers.
The air is still singed from Friday's fire on the ridge.
The lightest of its smoke crept through our windows,
left threads of ash on the sills, its incense caught in the curtains.

Arabic lessons in Egypt

At a masjid in Madinat Nasr,
just before Maghrib,
I find Jidatee with her nose
in His signs while a metronome
of bone on bone
keeps time.

With each fatha,
with each kasra,
she breathes,
and those knees creak
as much as the scuffed plastic
of the chair under them.

She's not really my grandmother.
I hear only one word out of her hundred.
Ana la atakalam arabiyya, the guidebook told me to say.
Ana talibah, min junoob iffrikiya, was from today's lesson.

Jidatee fingers the dark cloth of my jacket
then pointing to my skin, trying to ask:
South Africa but how, you are not black?
I stumble: Ummi's— ummi's— ummi min Hindeeyah.

(I haven't yet learnt the word for great-grandmother.)

Jidatee brings her finger to her forehead,
makes a little circle with it in the middle.
La, la, Muslim, I say. It sounds a bit like a song.
We laugh before we pray.

When I return home to my jidatee,
I tell her the words for jam, love and need
are the same as the ones in Gujarati.
I tell her all her prayers for me and the world

were already made in a mosque in Cairo.

The apartment

I've never met the neighbours
yet their lives leak through the walls
slipping in through the window
along with the theme from *Braveheart*
and the colicky baby
pee finding porcelain
two flushes
a cough some guitar chords
canned laughter bubbling under the paint.

Women on beaches

have always been explosive. The female body has a combined fission yield of ten nuclear islands. The first bathing suit was a wooden house wheeled into the sea. They used to sew weights into hemlines. Drowning was a kind of modesty. Policemen measured the lengths of bathing suits. The first bikini was made up of four fabric triangles in newspaper print. The female body is a lead headline. Réard said a bikini revealed everything about a girl except for her mother's maiden name. As if a women confesses through every pore, her secrets a sheen upon her skin. The female body is still contested territory. There are men defining these borders. A woman who is different is always dangerous. They arrested the first woman who swam without her wooden house. A woman who does not look like the other women must be hiding something. They stripped a woman for wearing too much. Policemen still measure the lengths of bathing suits.

My world today

No babies yet.
I am the heaviest I have ever been.
I do not pray as I should.
I am the Muslim at the gate.
White people are afraid.
I just want to be a mother.
I'm upset with God.
But I'm not ready to give it all up.

Boxing Day

Now you know I've written much
about fathers folded in cottoned fatiha,
camphored zikr, tasbeeh tongues.
There is only so much funerary
one can bear in a poem.

What we know for sure:
the living are here; the dead are not,
but become more than the day they left.

I once told someone when I write
it's not mine any more.
Over these years I have given
this day away to friends and strangers.
What is passed on is no longer held by the line.

In this soft caramel season

                                    we are in the thick of love.
Under secrets held by the rain, atop murmuring moss,
my meaty tongue curls under your watch. I pull
kitten skin from your neck, lick must from your mouth –
everything a glisten, everywhere a growl.
Listen for it: the shift, the clumping earth,
the slack of trees, the tense of muscle.

The good life

Good girls clean chickens
love their grannies
marry well
cry in cupboards
dust under dressers
don't visit empty-handed

Good girls want their children
go on beach holidays
Google recipes for red velvet
make biryani for fifty
thread just the bottom of their brows
make Jumu'ah lunch

Good girls come like in the movies
wax until they shine
swallow on demand
hum within reason
don't scratch their pots
put up with a hell of a lot

Hagiography

That you died when you did I don't mind any more.
At six, it was too much. At 29, I can take it.
Talk about perfect timing: I never got around to hating you.

The way I speak of you, incense offerings off my tongue.
You generous man, faultless, holding dolls who talk
when you push their hearts, day-glo dinosaur bones.

I wear your skinny Bob Marley ties and fedora,
your spongy ears soaking up sob-stories, fabled
and for-real. People say we're too soft

but we just like to listen. I no longer grudge
what you've passed on to me: your bold nose, this
clefted chin, the way our smiles make dashes for eyes.

It's like you had to go so I could take your place.

Our house is not child-friendly

Electric traps jut from the walls,
the perfect size for little fingers.
Our coffee table is violent,
an old bookcase waits to bury something.
The gynae points to the ultrasound –
there, the clusters of cysts.
In our house the steps to the garage
are steep and gateless.

Ectopic

Parents don't have to be parents
to hold things their children touch.

Almost Joburged

When I recount this story I verb this city into something
that'll shank you in places only a poem can plaster.
Or, in this incident, show you its stolen gun
in fair exchange for the phone you were foolish
to check in a brazen morning while in the car,
stopped at a robot surrounded by other cars
with other drivers similarly distracted.

You've got to look up to survive, I know this now,
and for sure give no fucks about who's coming up
in the lane next to you to get the hell away
from that gun blooming from under a torn T-shirt
in daylight so broad, it must be performance art.
But not today, my man, my city, not today:
my photos haven't synced to the cloud yet,

and there's no password on my lock screen.

Every single one of us

Every woman I know has something
crushed up in a piece of newspaper,
shoulder blades stung by bra straps,
a step between her step, tick-ticking in the dark.

The women I know can tell you
how a whisper cuts in a lift,
about the voices from unknown callers,
the nightmare of being awake.

Every woman I know can tell other women
they know stories of escape,
what numbers to have on speed-dial,
about the soft parts that stun when pressed.

We talk among ourselves.
We tell of our days
how we made it out okay, thank God.
Sometimes we're not so lucky.

I, the divine

after Rabih Alameddine

1
My hands
are not big enough
to grasp prayer,
my tongue not loose enough
to utter them.

2
When I prostrate
it is knees pressed
against chest,
forehead taped to the ground.
This sajdah is a sealed offering.

3
I take the wire from three paper clips
and shape them to look like
abstract forms in prayer.
As their pliancy moulds
into poses of submission,
so I sculpt the acceptance
of my form.

4
It is a godly act
to bend.

The fleamarket clown

We're at Bruma and I know this clown
from Saturday morning TV.
He asks for a kiss –
just one on his cheek –
and when I bend to him
he turns the trick.
There I meet his rubbery pout,
breath sugary with booze,
and needles, needles on my chin.

Plaits

We fail little girls by not
presenting them
with the alternatives. Think
of the waste that is a plait,

        pulled and
        oiled and
Love-in-Tokyo'd.

God handed down to us
the knowledge of scissors.
To think I could have been as free
as Abdul from across the road.

What am I to do

                        with these strange women
holding up dolls, bloodied on my screen,
unravelling mummies embalmed in dust,
pixels swaddled in strips of calico.

                        with crying fathers
and the bricks of bodies, the litter of limbs
strewn about feeds, filling the cache
behind my eyes at night. I dream of disc error.

                        when I put my brow
to the ground, and begin to download
or upload, or whatever it is we do
when we ask God to start over.

Ummah

The light in a heart
can be a stone in a hand.

Zikr makes a whole.
Takbeer becomes a cleaver.

Bend and break
five times a day.

No two are put together the same way.
I want you to be my brother, brother.

This faith can be a river.
It can also keep you damned.

By heart

As a child I learnt things off by heart.
Private angels worked under the skin of my chest
scratching prompts on pulsing tissue.

In the afternoons at madressah
I prayed with sounds from engraved organs,
repeating after the moulana Arabic letters
starting their lives in different parts of my throat.

Don't mix them up, he said.
You could be saying *dog* instead of *heart*.
The meanings of other things he did not teach,
crafting for us sacred chants only God would understand.

As an adult I had to look again to my heart,
the places the angels left, their tools scattered blindly.
I bent to pick one up.

The old woman barely moves

In this room the oxygen concentrator
is the only thing breathing with confidence.
The one certain chest to cave and peak,
lungs louder than prayers conditioning the air.

The eldest child must be bravest now
and remove the machine's pinching fingers,
read the down across her philtrum,
search for damp proof of being.

The other children cup their hands over hers
as if they were holding a baby bird.

Old man tears

In the middle of photographing children
smashing cake and trilling, when
you answer the phone and it says
I don't think I can go on any more.

You never learned how to deal with old man tears.
You keep the tone clinical:
Has the doctor been to your room?
It'll be OK once you're on the meds.

You disconnect, hope you've called the bluff.
The children swing cricket bats at the piñata.

You see him afterwards, discharged,
sunk, smaller than you remember,
perched on the edge of the bed
bone-bent, with the naked feet of a child.

Blusterless, a torn packet in the veld.
Salt tremoring his face as if
you've never heard that voice shake
a room and bring down the plaster.

Whatever flickered at the back of his eyes, snuffed.
The fury medicated. He is so much quieter now.

Kind regards

We are currently unable to supply the requisite level of grief.

At the time of writing, we have not finalised the format of our mourning. Given our sentiments towards the deceased in recent years it would not align with our values to display an excessive show of emotion.

We are aware that tears are expected and we will probably concede to some extent as an acquiescence to distant relatives in order to mitigate their bereavement. You must understand this is a complicated issue and will require some further consideration before a final decision can be made.

Burning rituals for New Year

That particular smell of hair on fire,
dead, but life itself is singeing, sweet and acid in one lick.
I know someone who burns to clear her energies.
My people tend to bury instead, they say.

Never put the crescents of your nails or past blood
in the bin, someone could use your biology against you.
I don't care for dark ways, just how best to honour
what we discard of ourselves, willingly or not.

All the things hair remembers, the proof of where we're from.

Biodata

Not your silken swish, I don't froth when I whisper.
I am not the coolness of your eye, or any kind of pearl
underneath a cape. I don't take sugar. I can't mend time.
I don't trust the wind. I won't make exceptions for kites.

I am the howl of the dogs after midnight.
The dash on the last line, the hole in your pocket.
I am what the sun began. I take my ghosts to the movies.
Find meaning in the corners. I hold coals and don't flinch.

I won't pack sand around your heart. I will fill your mouth with zephyrs.
I will leave a bomb in your hand and quietly close the door.

Breakdown

One quarter of you sits in the lounge in sun-striped flannel pyjama pants
eating watermelon from a tub. Half a man less, or some other fraction
of who you were this time last year. I know the mind can be uncertain.
Who can trust the day when the night is just a fall away, when regret is a qareen
that sits with you, squeezing your soft parts until you tear up and plead?

You are the child we never had: tantrums on the kitchen floor,
as bald as any baby, perhaps a slight more manipulative.

Comings of age

The first time I ate an ant, it tasted sharp against my tongue. The first time I bled from the head was when it connected with the back of a swing at Zoo Lake. I looked white enough to get into the hospital ward but my name turned them against me. There was another hospital, and my first x-ray. I looked up at a light, my neck cradled by a pillow filled with beans. The second time I bled from the head, I fell off the back of a truck. The first boy who liked me first drove a purple Beetle, called me every night and it was so boring. The first boy I liked looked like Michael J Fox. We had a high school English teacher who was perpetually pregnant. I ate fish cakes after attending my first Christian funeral. At my uncle's funeral, I remember thinking how odd must God think us, Muslims at a service for a Catholic man at a Hindu crematorium. The first time I ate oysters, I didn't know it was cruel to chew them. They pull back in their shells when you poke them. Tip back and swallow, better stomach acid than the gnash of teeth. My father tried to teach me chess. I learnt the names of the pieces and their positions on the board. He died before I learnt their moves. I played draughts with my grandfather. When my grandfather started using machines for breath, I would lay out his clothes every evening for the next day until there wasn't one. He had three tiered hangers for organising his trousers by colour. His room smelt like rosewater and leg wounds. My grandmother smoked cigarettes only when it rained. I once asked my mother what sex was all about and she said it's when a man and a woman get close. I used to skim through copies of Mills & Boons at the public library just to get to the scenes.

Birds of prey

Certain hawks in Australia drop flaming twigs on dry areas
to scare out their food with the fires.
This is the only way he knows how.

He holds a match to your skin and waits.
You walk from room to room holding fish in your jaw.
I come from women who stayed

because of what they thought people would say.
The children of these men hate having their picture taken
because photographs are too honest about lineage.

Golden hour

The uncle selling books outside Hanover Bakery says people are going every day.
I know. I've seen it for myself. One day here, and then you're just not.
On a not-day I walk among the red mounds that are the Muslim graves, some
with names stencilled on green perspex and prayers for the best of the Hereafter.
Some flaunt more adamant supplications, others staked with plywood,
scratched into like plant markers on the succulent beds.

Sectioned like this, categorised by faith, you might say in death too we choose
to lie with our own. If you did happen to call God by the right name
there'd be no rubbing your neighbour's time-cleaned nasal bone
in any more dirt than they'd become accustomed to.
There is afternoon sun stuttering through the pines, flashing slides.
We could picnic in your cemetery, if I could find you here.

I see a man, prayer book in hand, standing at a grave so still, he could be carved.
As much as I try, the leaves are still crackling under my feet.

Learning to pray

Alif, the first letter, pronounce it *a leaf.*
This is how we wrote to memory.

Muslims who didn't speak Arabic or understand it,
but who could say it and read it,
we learnt ways around it, praying by ear.
Meaning would come later, if ever.

Qul Huw-Allahu Ahad.
Say He God Is One.
Cool who will law who a had.
Say He God is One.

Allah-us-Samad.
God is All-Embracing.
All law who sam add.
God is all-embracing.

Secret

We were eight when you made me hold your secret.
You knit my skin, fused my fingers around it. I promised.
I kept a copy of it under my tongue for safekeeping.
But there is always the struggle of clay expanding in moist conditions.
What doesn't slip down the throat swells up in the mouth.

Facebook tells me you're a good mother now.
It's been so many years since but I need to tell you now
I want to see your children paint a wall with their palm prints,
I want to see their tonsils when they laugh.
But it is too late for us. We should have broken open years ago.

It wasn't our shame to carry in our fists.
It was the monster's, from the caffee we never went back to.

Khushoo

The birds of paradise on my musalla
don't have faces because I was told
the angels of mercy won't visit if they did,
and it would interfere with my concentration anyway.

But here I am in rukū' staring at the image
of a bird with wings and no beak, but flowers
that look like pouty mouths, and I think about how
our parents probably kissed before their wedding.

But no one tells us these things.
I shouldn't be pondering this in the middle of salah.
This must be Shaytaan at it again,
but didn't I read taawuz at the start?

I seek refuge in Allah from Satan, the Accursed.
All my life I've prayed in this patchwork,
stretches of doubt in a loop of desertscape.
I've offered up more apologies than awe.

But when my Ashadu Allah finger moves
up and down like a sewing needle
I feel I'm being stitched together with
someone else, who at this moment

could be looking down at their prayer mat,
wondering how these birds will find their nests.

Ummi

Softer than stone and stronger has run
between Safa and Marwa for as long I breathe.
She has lived five times over moving
from mountain to mountain carrying
my heart above her own.

A mother's song is lament and prayer.

2

I slept on the shoulders of her lullabies stitched
with Shahaadah, her Allahu Allahu
wound around the thumb in my mouth.
In the car we rode to Tracy Chapman, Dolly Parton,
on the back of the Buffalo Soldier.

We sang together until I grew to the age
where a musical mother is embarrassing.
I switched off the radio.

A mother's song is loss and yearning.

3
Still in those fumbling, static years
she kicked up dust, searched for water in the valleys,
waiting for the slow sloughing sandpaper
of time to soften our notes.
Till the day my parched throat cracked

and from it a voice like her own deep resonance –
on key, just slightly off-pitch,
a song that carried and carried.

At my mother's feet gushed
the springs of home and hereafter.

GLOSSARY

ana la atakalam arabiyya: *I don't speak Arabic*
ana talibah, min junoob iffrikiya: *I am a student from South Africa*
fatha: in Arabic script, the vowel point for *a*
fatiha: a prayer; the first chapter of the Quran
jidatee: *my grandmother*
kasra: in Arabic script, the vowel point for *i*
la la: *no, no*
Madinat Nasr: a suburb in Cairo
maghrib: the sunset prayer
min Hindeeya: *from India*
tasbeeh: a rosary
ummi: *my mother*
zikr: the remembrance of God

POETRY FOR THE PEOPLE

— AVAILABLE NOW —

In a Free State and *Foundling's Island* by P.R. Anderson

White Blight by Athena Farrokhzad, translated by Jennifer Hayashida
IN ASSOCIATION WITH ARGOS BOOKS, USA

Milk Fever by Megan Ross

Liminal by Douglas Reid Skinner

Collective Amnesia by Koleka Putuma
CITY PRESS BOOK OF THE YEAR 2017

Thungachi by Francine Simon

Modern Rasputin by Rosa Lyster

Prunings by Helen Moffett
CO-WINNER OF THE 2017 SOUTH AFRICAN
LITERARY AWARD FOR POETRY

Questions for the Sea by Stephen Symons
HONOURABLE MENTION FOR THE
2017 GLENNA LUSCHEI PRIZE FOR AFRICAN POETRY

Failing Maths and My Other Crimes by Thabo Jijana
WINNER OF THE 2016 INGRID JONKER PRIZE FOR POETRY

Matric Rage by Genna Gardini
COMMENDED FOR THE 2016 INGRID JONKER PRIZE FOR POETRY

the myth of this is that we're all in this together by Nick Mulgrew

AVAILABLE FROM GOOD BOOKSTORES IN SOUTH AFRICA
& FROM THE AFRICAN BOOKS COLLECTIVE ELSEWHERE

UHLANGAPRESS.CO.ZA

Printed in the United States
By Bookmasters